Flower Conroy's exquisite language is like a fierce storm, a tasty bite of forbidden fruit (which, we learn, and instantly believe, might have been *quince*…). Seduction, in her skilled hands, is adventure, is danger, sports colorful red lips, fuchsia shoes. To read Flower Conroy is to be taken apart, sliced open, seared with lightning.

Laura Foley author of *Joy Street* and *The Glass Tree*

In *The Awful Suicidal Swans,* even the weather transmits damage or indifference; lightning cracks like a ribcage; the cold closes in. These are not comforting poems and clearly, Flower Conroy does not mean them to be. They should come with the warning *read at your own risk,* though you should take the chance. There is both rage and remarkably beautiful language within these dark verses that will leave the reader with a new perspective on the power of poetry itself.

Eleanor Lerman author of *Strange Life* and *The Sensual World Re-Emerges*

Fashioning imagery from the gorgeous to the gritty, Flower Conroy conjures moments of lust, love, and life with power and passion. Like the tattoos that crop up now and again in these lines, her poems leave an indelible mark on the mind.

Leila J. Rupp author of *Sapphistries: A Global History of Love Between Women*

These formally immaculate, sonically rich poems overflow with grit and perfume—with patent leather and Redwoods, laundromats and apple clover, Lucky Strikes and overripe eggplant. The abstract becomes tangible, tasteable, and the enormous turns microscopic as Conroy explores the wildness of the erotic. With stormy, charged language and a disarming directness, the poems ask, again and again, *How alive are you?* In this extraordinary chapbook, Conroy shows us how to be more alive, more animal, and more human.

Alyse Knorr author of *Annotated Glass*

Flower Conroy is like Marianne Moore punch-drunk in love with a pole dancer. Each poem in this book pays gorgeous attention to sound as it careens after the body through bars, blizzards, and memories. *The Awful Suicidal Swans* is a "Kiss, apocalypse" that will leave you breathless.

Rita Mae Reese author of *The Alphabet Conspiracy*

The Awful Suicidal Swans

The Awful Suicidal Swans

Flower Conroy

HEADMISTRESS PRESS

Copyright © 2014 by Flower Conroy
All rights reserved.

ISBN-13: 978-0692264386
ISBN-10: 0692264388

This book may not be reproduced, in whole or in part, including illustrations, in any form (beyond that permitted by Sections 107 and 108 of the U.S. Copyright Law and except by reviewers for the public press), without written permission from the publishers.

Front cover photo © Bas Meelker, www.123rf.com
Back cover photo of Flower Conroy © 2011 by Nick Doll

Cover & book design by Mary Meriam

PUBLISHER
Headmistress Press
60 Shipview Lane
Sequim, WA 98382
Telephone: 917-428-8312
Email: headmistresspress@gmail.com
Website: headmistresspress.blogspot.com

for VLM

Contents

In the Wolf's Den * Gentlemen's Club	1
Me, Me Not	2
Prime	3
Angel of Meat, Eye of the Past	4
The Podophiliac	5
Abraded Hour Above the Laundromat	6
Your Body the Unnameable Body	7
God Trace	8
Whiteout	10
Development	12
How did the Everlasting Begin?	13
At Lucy's Flaming Lips Bar	14
An Offering of Throat	15
Corporal Pleasance	16
Shadow Animalia Lullaby	17
Lepus Chasing Lupus	18
Of Exaltations	19

With Exception to Flight & Tickling	20
Unquenching	21
Brontophobia	22
Juxtaposition Among Redwoods	24
Again, Rain	25
Granting Passage	26
Signature Heat	28
You've Been Bit by a Dangerous Snake	29
Paisley bruise on her shoulder, same astonished green	30
Achexquisite	31
Therefore I am	32
The Morning After	33
Body Remembrance	34
Acknowledgments	37
About the Author	39

In the Wolf's Den * Gentlemen's Club

Swatches of black light glinted off her patent
leather pumps, daggers of sun. Drum & guitar
growled from speakers, subwoofer throbbed.

Redd's untied fur-trimmed cloak slipped into a blood-
colored puddle at her heels. You were in love all over
again—strawberry blond April—you could see it in her

eyes, you had not seen her in years—revamped: platinum
pageboy wig, razor blade features, claw & claw mark
tattoo on her alabaster hip threatening

to snip the knot of her scarlet string bikini.
She pouted her candy-apple lacquer lips, paced
the platform then sprung. Nonchalant she hung, hooked

by her leg, upside-down from polished chrome.
She tossed vague rose-petal stares into the shadow-
blotted lair. Reinvented, unraveled, she strutted

lamblike across the stage; stopped as if she recognized
the song or something she shouldn't forget,
then dipped down, legs bowed, pulverized

the smoke thick air, then inched back up. You, in love,
on the playground, spinning April on the merry-
go-round, untamed laugh, poppy field of freckles,

head thrown back as the sky turned... They panted,
howled, wagged. She scoured the room. *Encore. Encore.*
Crumpled money-flowers littered, littered the floor.

Me, Me Not

Not a contrived still life, but as if I hid
in a field behind a giant bloom, efflorescence obscured.

Tepals, skin & sepals. *Petrichor*—scent of rain on garland,
on dust, my breath & the word

for blood in the mouth is *hesitate*. Is *ichor*. My face
a giant flower. If I could be reborn something beautiful.

You vacillate, plucking my heartstrings, *does she/
does she not…* Orchid wicked, or fringed in cones.

Steeped in eucalyptus. Or among the apple clover.
You alone in a corn field reveal your corolla.

Behind you, the sun, a candle wrapped in paper.

Prime

In the abandoned meat factory, rain grizzled
the stairwell. He was shirtless,
cardboard beneath you.
Beyond the cinderblocks, breath
of traffic, industrial & silver. Clouds
within clouds, the yellow leaves
lining October. Upside-down
? hooks dangled
from the ceiling. Out
of body. That is, beyond yourself.
Beyond what you thought you were
capable of. The rusty fan scraped
in its cell. Later that night, ribcage
of lightning, pulse of storm.
That place no longer exists,
bulldozed, condemned, a lot
of nothing & busted bottles.
You recall its other names: The Beef Barn.
Abattoir. Slaughterhouse. When you left,
you left nameless, carrying your shoes.

Angel of Meat, Eye of the Past

In the lobby of the Ray Caesar, a girl eats an orange.
Shovels orange in her calamity mouth, orange bit
after orange bit, cheeks swollen with pulp. Rind fragments
litter her lap. Her flat-line stare infinities through window,
through you. Double-edged sword night.
This nocturnal dress. These gouged stockings.
Skin peeks through silk.
New heels, scuffed. Punched
one-way ticket night. Night of halos.
Girl eating an orange in the lobby
of the Ray Caesar night while you stagger
through sizzling rain night,
night of neither silence
nor salvation; night, violet unblinking night.

The Podophiliac

What wouldn't you do, walking that fine-
line I never understood anyway,
toeing *what it is to be desire
incarnate,* to be wanted? Now you wanted
to disappear, you flipped through his skin-rag
stash, all those *fuck me* glances
staring into the camera & coming off
the high-gloss pages while he promised to worship you
from the ankles
down.

Abraded Hour Above the Laundromat

You swabbed your armpits
with a crumpled washcloth
that reeked
of the ozone. Paper-
chain of bruises where you were held
onto like gravity.
Will it always be like this? Chemical
perfume. Steam & starch, the feral
hiss of the machines as they pressed
empty gowns & empty coats.
You spit
clean the smudges
underscoring
your iron-blue
scorched *YES* eyes.

Your Body the Unnameable Body

If I were on the other side of that steam-cloaked glass
with you, I would touch your edges. I'd cup
the bars of your ribs.
Feel how they feel against
my fingers' dragging, a scalloped frame,
a warped archway. A harp.

    I am almost afraid of you.

Collapsed on the couch, the curtain
moving slowly like a moth breathing.
You coming back, your body a statue
against the murk.

Towel-drying your hair.

You. Now I remember.
The owl ascending from hell
and descending into a patch of chanterelle.
You, leaving
wet footprints. Ghost of an angel
wrapped in ivy. Mascara
smeared eyes. You.

The dark air
inside a sleigh bell.

God Trace

Eve pressed her gun
to your shoulder.
A white whiskered dragon clawed
up from her thin jeans, sinking
its milky talons into her ribcage.
Her machine stirred
below your surface,

its hum conjured: a crushed hive
or a boot's breaking of a book's binding.
You struck a match, lit a Lucky
Strike, inhaled smoke as if breathing in the dust
of an angel then offered
it to her. She took it between her patent leather lips

& continued stitching flesh tapestry with fluid thread.
Buds of dew blossomed, blood pooled
from the emerging tattoo. With a rag she smeared red
across your arched back's sun starved skin.
With her mouth she smeared red
across your famished mouth.

I could no longer watch through the basement
window. I relinquished—your image embedded
in my mind, a stain. I crossed
the streets, sought the sanctuary of my car.
Eve forward & backwards, branding
your back, Eve crying
out, her dragon dancing.

The car engine vibrated against the cold.
I drove without destination,
passed a billboard that promised:
Jesus Saves. Marveled
how the difference between a cross & a
crucifix was a man. How the difference

between sacrifice & sacrilege
could be dissolved into suffixation.
And ultimately, how one difference
may make all the difference. Like if it were one
degree colder there'd be the possibility tonight
for indifferent snow.

Whiteout

A winter storm darkens homes,
disrupts travel, lingers like a girl pacing
a corner. Random streets glow,

glazed with streetlamps' golden haze. Quilts
of wet snow mute cars into humps,
power failures stain windows.

The jaundice-tinged trees' branchy
tentacles, bearing the weight of snowflake
mutilated into bank of scar tissue,

conjures Dirk Fuchs' ninety-five-million-
year old ultraviolet *Octopus vulgaris*.
The delicate construction

of the octopod's antiquated fossil—
a film upon the seafloor like toothpaste
scum drying on the sink edge

or the sculpture of a sneeze.
The prostitute leans into the cracked
window of a sedan. One man has been killed

by a fallen bough in Central Park
but the real threat is that strong
winds will create blizzard conditions.

Already it has spread
a fire that glitched from an oceanfront
hotel into the games arcade beside it.

She slides onto the front seat,
unzips the paleobiologist's starched pants.
Fetches from the gaping linen, the planted

squid & milks it, warm, aglow udder, invisible
ink, muffled mantra, & behind her
eyes, a fury of flurries, cold thoughts.

Development

Once, beyond the chain link fence,
a thicket of wilderness. The gravel

company's skyline of sand spires
hourglassing the horizon. Silt

accumulated in the windowsills
& March, especially, wind'd take fistfuls

of invisible granules & whiplashes
them into your hair, your mouth.

Sometimes, a singular sharp grain
riding air, would jackknife

into an open eye. The blood-
root, poison ivy, wild red Columbine:

uprooted & trucked away.
Machinery has felled the trees,

now exposing through the diamonds
of the fence, a cleared shrubland.

The train's unbuffered yowl rattles
the complex as if it means to cleave clean

through. You left for the last time. That empty
slash of sky? A gray wound. Chance of hail.

How did the Everlasting Begin?

Kiss, apocalypse. Body, a configuration of myriad fiber-
glass threads & a pair of eyes broken into/*hysteria in the soul.*
It began with a wrist. The wrist touched a hand. The hand held
itself to the fire. There was nothing spectacular about the fire, its orange
smoke slithered into the hungry ether. The wood went from young
to bone. It began with a look. The flexing
shadow of a sundial. *In each fiber of the body.*
The wrist of the rosebush. The somethousand petals, the 2
billion stars. How lonely you stood miniaturized in the overgrowth.
When the flashfloods thrash the landscape, it is the clouds' fault.
There was everything spectacular about the fire
because it was ordinary.
Because it was contained
& then it was not.

At Lucy's Flaming Lips Bar

—I don't know if I'll make it home tonight but I know I can swim under the Tahitian moon—Porno for Pyros

A tattoo for each of your lovers
& at your ankle, calligraphy
of slashes, of *tricks*. Jukebox mewing

You don't belong here. I wouldn't go near you.
Didn't want you to see me
looking at you. Had to pass

you on the way to The Pisser.
Only one stall had a door
& it didn't lock. When I swung it open,

you stood there, *What's your problem bitch.*
I couldn't answer. *You deaf.*
Another girl fixing her eyeliner said, *Don't mess*

with her honey, she's scared of you, & it
took me a moment to figure out she was
talking to me. But you

already had a fistful of my hair
& you cut my lip open bringing my mouth
to yours. Smudge of blood called *fire-kissed.*

An Offering of Throat

Are you suggesting no one has proposed,
Your divine throat begs the simplicity
of a diamond solitaire or a strand of

pearl-colored pearls? Are you implying that men
& women don't lean over your shoulder,
lean close into your abundant auburn curls

hypnotized by your milky neck, its bright
sculpture pleading to be bit? I relish how,
when you lecture or first-smile, it trembles.

As if your heart were caged there amidst
unspoken words. Vehicle to your lips.
So when you cover it as you often do

in scarf or collar, I think it a subconscious
act, like the endangered Bengal tigress
parading its zoo room,

dreaming in Bangladesh, dreaming
in black & white, dreaming in
wild & hunger & tiger.

Corporal Pleasance

Crop of warped shadows: skullcap—lungwort—heart-
wood—& bleeding heart. *I invite you in...* suspires
the dreamt garden, offspring of paradise;
your wicked entrails mushroom succulents,
belladonnas, splinter flowers. Amidst the slow-gulping
fringe-mouths of Venus flytraps,
you peel back the layers of your skin. Witness
the thistles' subtle dance. Cry of cherry jubilee.
Some believe the forbidden fruit, you pluck
a planetary orb mantled in gray fuzz, *was not apple,
but quince.* I bite astringent meat & fall
back into a cocoon of leaves but not before
a thorn—with its single, deft stroke—like the opening
of a letter—fingernails my cheek.

Shadow Animalia Lullaby

Sun twisted loose: a chill of pine & mist, unleashed,
snaked us. In woods' belly, boughs crumbled
into cellulose. Quill-like twigs snapped;
skullcap crushed underfoot. *You'll be swallowed by
dark if you leave.* The pallescent, encroaching
moonlight, which you eased into, spilled through the foliage
like snowfall, dissolved like snowfall.
I lit the firepit. Thought: *let the flames' false balladry
seduce me.* Moth allure, slow burning match.
You look like a doll, you breathed, *a gypsy tart,
a ruby-collared hummingbird.* You traced my face, then my hair.
Underbreath: *you smell of merlot, tobacco, a city
after rain.* Behind your wall of teeth, murmuration.
Above, the satellites wallowed in their brilliant hollow
but I could no longer recall. *What took you so long?*

Lepus Chasing Lupus

Rickety cabin sinking into Ozark. The wind
sounded apologetic & the dream
catchers, webbed with sea
glass & bone, woven by brides of St. Francis
dangled from the porch's eave.
Internally I was equinox, I was meteor frantic,
ransacked into planetary bloom. Scattered
pitter-patter of acorns pelting tin roof, hard
dirt, then the sudden glance of ghost-eyes
from a doe—exposed when the back door opened
behind me & the colossal light from the kitchen
shone into the yard & your arms encased me
& I followed you down
into a hole & your mouth burrowed into my hair,
prey preying on prey, breaths
of mercy, of immateriality, *good…*
good…
too good.
I.

Of Exaltations

Below the lovers' suite, *The Broken
Cloud,* frenzy of butterflies & gnats.

Beyond the collapsing
fence the orchard's apply ever after air,

the virescent pond submitting
to its sublime, dragonfly death.

Possessed as Podkowinski's manic stallion
(whose equine portrait hangs above the headboard),

tremblings, *The Swollen Bite,* crickets
Kama Sutra in the grass' understory,

for the first time, the colt tastes its bit.
While in the overflowing garden, corn rots, overripe

eggplant split, cabbage surrender to deer.
Coral & Jewel, gardenia loll. Here ends love's

different kinds of sampling, thigh resting on thigh.
Glazed lovers, hay smell of bliss filling your nostrils,

the razing crop, do you never wonder
who will feed the chickens?

With Exception to Flight & Tickling

The only feather
of significance is this brown & white quill I

dip & scribe down the length
of your shivering dreamy molted body:

hot blue skin calligraphy;
haikus
of unspeakable desires.

Unquenching

Mind dipped in fairy-tale slumber—crystal formation
within the disc of an erupting star—you dreamt
        upon ocean, rocked into nap by liquid arms—
Andromeda ship's unexplored cradle.

I sponged afternoon, absorbed the view: across water's
surface sunshine dazzled—mercury beading with each
        wave's blistering, hypnosis of drowning
unremembered kaleidoscopic warped pattern.

Yesterday I overheard a stranger call the blue of this met-
amorphous pool *miraculous* & I contemplated:
        stars' dark star wombs; blue-green atmosphere;
cosmic seeds dividing; sprouts sprouting; that

succulent sound. I imagined vineyards lifting smog veils
with damp fingers; I concocted waterfalls of lava
        thickly smudging jungle mountainsides
of a curled, rooted island—then coagulating

into beds of cobalt ash. Dusty dead stars. The color
of the post-equinox. The hemispheric longitude
        of Venus. Lunar mountains.
You sighed. I ached to steal a sip of your lips…but my

drizzle touch awoke you. Beheld by archipelago, sunspot-
flecked satellite eyes—they mirrored volcanic firebody
        so that I swallowed deep, thirst-struck, whet for you,
while the world surrounding lapped patiently
against the parched, evaporating infrared aghast light.

Brontophobia

A couture sky adonized
in cloud cameos, charcoal & pearl
fastened to a bolt of dove

smog silk. We splurged.
Two dozen aubergine carnations gloved
in newspaper.   Piquant traffic. High

on the luxury
of being
alive in a city abandoned

by gods. We slipped in & out
of cafés, sipped Bordeaux, pondered
the gargoyles picking

their noses or flashing
teeth from spouts. Our boot-heels bit
into the cobblestone. Handsome

Venus, we crossed
the cemetery's threshold,
navigated avenues of the dead.

Black oak silhouettes
& inky tombstones backlit
by rust-tinged evening.

Later, at the restaurant, the storm
that sky promised beat its chest.
Twice electricity froze.

Candlelight lit our dishes. You ordered:
blue-veined cheese; cured meats
sliced into film; glazed roast duck

served on a bed of white
asparagus. And amidst the pouring
wine & chatter, we dined in yeasty dark—

linguini & bread crust, dipped in oil,
as downpour bellowed, & you
fed me & I, you.

Juxtaposition Among Redwoods

They were not red. Not as in blood-
red nails. Not red like apples, or corvettes.
These mythological bodies, thriving upward,
were welted rust, paprika-dusted, owl-
brown, tigered in moss. They whispered shadows.
This excursion before touring the vineyards.
You wore a leather trench coat. I teetered
along the pathway in fuchsia shoes.
Alone along some trail, separated from human
eyes, you took me to you with one arm,
& with the other, a singular
fallen limb. Said into my neck, *turn around* &
I did. The sky opened small enough for a cloud to escape.
It sounded like falling leaves, still clenched in branches.

Again, Rain

Ax amputating wood.
& the trashing swans

in the lake—
ignited muscle.

You wipe your brow
at the shadow of me.

You shudder in the cool shower;
my body decides

this is being skinned alive.
You hold me under

falling water. When you look
at me: kaleidoscopic pleasance.

Still: I see the languid necks
of birds limp as stockings.

I see kindle piling, waiting
for its witch, its match, a sulfur kiss.

My tied hands.
Under my tongue, a pearl.

Not a true pearl. Outside,
the awful suicidal swans.

The flapping sound of weather.
Pelt against skin.

Rain against rain.

Granting Passage

Leather dark polished
nails behold: me. To your blessing
bestowing mouth.

Therefore I am: crucified-
open, starfish-splayed.
Begging for drink. Begging

for fountain.
Will I or won't I come;
your patient blind-

worming. Can I harness
the redblack sky
of my mind, the red-

black birds
of thought, redblack clouds building
behind my eyelids, the

redblack trees' redblack branches
into my teeth's nerves,
my tongue's dirt road

of taste buds, can I amass
the redblack red, concentrate it
into one flame, one focal point

& hold it
there long enough for
you to cross & cross

the bridge,
that like night, is
this body?

Signature Heat

Arms pinned, slumber-warm sheets. Breathed
my hair in, my clavicle, inhaled the lair of my epidermis.
Tongue charmed armpit. Axilla, attar of: zodiac
& mink; souring milk; indigenous root, dark bed-
rock, & copper. Underarm: beds of pheromone, glands.
Calendula voodoo. Your tongue lands in the interior
of my shoulder; pocket of forested skin, muscles,
ball & socket. Were we any more animal, arousing sun
to shed her oily husks, we'd know each other only
by trail of musk. Any affection likewise: an act of primal
spot & recognition. You suckle the hollow. We find
ourselves in the gut of the quarry. Animal drawn,
come to lap from a starry shallow puddle, private trough.
Before you turn upon me, wild released one.

You've Been Bit by a Dangerous Snake

Switchblade cleavage, Cajun evening:
the charged Orleans' Saturday-night streets—
all florescence, spice & grime. *My brain's on fire, is
your brain on fire, too?*

Bangs stuck to my forehead like blades
of grass. Even the asphalt slithers.
Ubiquitous music. Feet
numb in heels not yet broken-in.
Dress clinging to my stomach with sweat, we

swagger-stagger back to the hotel, lured by cool
pillows & cut fruit. *Would you like to taste alternative
reality, the counterpoison to now?* With
a scarf, you cover my eyes. Reaching,
I hold onto the drapes.
Now; let me siphon that bite for you

says forked tongue, meaning, *little
Medusa, let me draw daggers from your heart.*

Paisley bruise on her shoulder, same astonished green

snaking behind her pupils. Limbs adorned with fresh welts
of ink. I kiss her smudged mouth & sludge-lined eye-
lids. Without her narcotic sweat, her voodoo breath
breathing down my neck, how did I survive? She ushers
me into her boudoir, steals my soul as collateral.
I feel as if I'm falling—she pushes me below the waterline.
She moves the hair from my face—this is why I dis-
appeared—she slaps my face with her mouth—this is why
I've returned—she examines my eyes—this the reason
I left in the first place. Then my she-devil hikes
up her leg—drags out her bow—extracts
a crucial song—punish- & replenishment, again & again
from the small body of her lovesick violin.

Achexquisite

I'd forgotten the hyssop aftertaste of paisley. Background
of nostalgia's strange piano sounds. I distinguish
your voice in the ripped velvet dark. I swore
I wouldn't: *the dark, the dark, the dark* but this glass
of dark makes me think of dark,
& more dark. How the thin shade
barely kept back the world outside. In the ceiling's mirror,
I was a skinned animal fastened by my own fascination
of you circling me: *Who lives
like this?* & *How alive are you?*

How   one

        body fit   the   other   with   a   little

muscle &

        some spit.

Therefore I am

on the floor in worship
position knees tucked
tergum   sculpture
of spine
cross of shoulder blades
cradle of hips & arms
outstretched in the moments
it takes you
to reach me
hours fountain
in my brain
blood bombards my ears
like being underwater
near a waterfall
of lava my insides turn
to gloss
when fields are torched
to prevent wild-
fires it is an act known as
controlled burn
when bamboo traces
where shadow
meets skin
the phoenix's wings burst
a rose
window the body
of my thoughts
shatter through

The Morning After

How the sun elbowed into the room.
Unrecognizable morning-
washed wallpaper, the scrolled
furniture buttery with day.
Breakfast's aroma unshackled me from sleep's
fantasies. Applewood, eggs Benedict,
roasted beans. Gardenia blooms
in a clear bowl. Fast.
As in, does not eat. As in happens
quickly. As in you un-
fastened my mouth with your mouth.
Cologne of last night, neon
summer, pink cocktails &
cigars, your thick & orchid hair.
So close leaning to me, I thought you'd singe me
with the coffee press. You pushed my bangs
from my eyes, put a cup in my hands
& commanded, *sip*.

Body Remembrance

I gave birth to your fist—
egg of flesh & bone
knuckles & collapsed

palm. Your grasp
fell from my nest
a semiprecious stone.

Hand hatched &
emerged as a tulip
or crushed starfish

though I could not
look for in the moment
of release it spread

deep & took flight.
Slowly. As slowly
as you unfurled,

my eyes bloomed.
Days later I will still ache—
your phantom cradle

rocking within the boughs
of my womb, the emptiness
you created will reside

between thighs & there will be
no way to forget how once it
was buried & then it was born.

Acknowledgments

The following poems first appeared (sometimes in various incarnations) in these wonderful journals:

Blast Furnace: "Shadow Animalia Lullaby"
Cactus Heart: "How did the Everlasting Begin?"
Cliterature: "Whiteout" and "Brontophobia"
Horror Sleaze Trash: "Prime," "Of Exaltations," "Juxtaposition Among Redwoods" and "Achexquisite"
Jelly Bucket: "Again, Rain"
Labletter: "Into the Wolf's Den * Gentlemen's Club"
Lavender Review: "Granting Passage" and "Corporal Pleasance"
Menacing Hedge: "Angel of Meat, Eye of the Past"
Penduline: "Abraded Hour Above the Laundromat," "Signature Heat" and "Paisley bruise on her shoulder, same astonished green"
Plenitude: "You've Been Bit by a Dangerous Snake"
Psychic Meatloaf: "Your Body the Unnameable Body"
Saw Palm: "Unquenching" and "The Morning After"
Serving House Journal: "An Offering of Throat"
Sunsets & Silencers: "God Trace"
The Moose & The Pussy: "Body Remembrance"

I would like to thank my family and friends for supporting my writing and encouraging me to follow my dreams—*you know who you are and I love you!*

I would also like to acknowledge and thank my mentors, especially Cat Doty for believing in me from the beginning; Renee Ashley, David Daniel, and Kathy Graber at Fairleigh Dickinson University for their insight and guidance; Laura McCullough for having my back; and the many incredible instructors I've had the honor of studying with at various writing conferences and whose knowledge has helped shape my development as a poet (including but certainly not limited to): Kazim Ali; Michael Collier; Forrest Gander; Linda Gregerson; Robert Hass; Brenda Hillman; Sally Keith; Katharyn Howd Machan; Peter Murphy; Sharon Olds; Mary Jo Salter; Evie Shockley; A. E. Stallings; Mark Strand; Mary Szybist.

Laura Foley, Alyse Knorr, Eleanor Lerman, Rita Mae Reese, and Leila Rupp—sincere gratitude for your keen readings and generous words. *Thank you!!!*

A huge heartfelt THANK YOU goes out to Risa Denenberg and Mary Meriam of Headmistress Press for loving these poems and getting them into the world—their guidance, enthusiasm, and unfaltering support has been instrumental in not only shaping this collection, but in making it a reality. *Ladies, thank you.*

Lucy.

I thank and am thankful for my partner, Vicki—*what would I do without you in my life?? Your inexhaustible belief and encouragement that what I'm doing is worthwhile keeps me writing and aspiring to write better. This is for you. Now let's make more poetry!*

About the Author

Originally from New Jersey, Flower Conroy currently lives in Key West, Florida, where she works as an esthetician. She earned her MFA from Fairleigh Dickinson University. Her first chapbook, *Escape to Nowhere* was selected as first runner-up in the Ronald Wardall Poetry Prize and was published by Rain Mountain Press. In addition to attending Bread Loaf, Tin House, Sewanee, and other writing conferences, she was awarded the Galway Kinnell Scholarship by Squaw Valley Writers' Conference, as well as a scholarship to attend Napa Valley Writers' Conference. Her poetry has won the Jeanette Gottlieb Poetry award, and has been published or is forthcoming in *American Literary Review, Poydras Review, Serving House Journal, Jai Alia, Sierra Nevada Review,* and other journals.

Headmistress Press Books

Lovely - Lesléa Newman
Teeth & Teeth - Robin Reagler
How Distant the City - Freesia McKee
Shopgirls - Marissa Higgins
Riddle - Diane Fortney
When She Woke She Was an Open Field - Hilary Brown
God With Us - Amy Lauren
A Crown of Violets - Renée Vivien tr. Samantha Pious
Fireworks in the Graveyard - Joy Ladin
Social Dance - Carolyn Boll
The Force of Gratitude - Janice Gould
Spine - Sarah Caulfield
Diatribe from the Library - Farrell Greenwald Brenner
Blind Girl Grunt - Constance Merritt
Acid and Tender - Jen Rouse
Beautiful Machinery - Wendy DeGroat
Odd Mercy - Gail Thomas
The Great Scissor Hunt - Jessica K. Hylton
A Bracelet of Honeybees - Lynn Strongin
Whirlwind @ Lesbos - Risa Denenberg
The Body's Alphabet - Ann Tweedy
First name Barbie last name Doll - Maureen Bocka
Heaven to Me - Abe Louise Young
Sticky - Carter Steinmann
Tiger Laughs When You Push - Ruth Lehrer
Night Ringing - Laura Foley
Paper Cranes - Dinah Dietrich
On Loving a Saudi Girl - Carina Yun
The Burn Poems - Lynn Strongin
I Carry My Mother - Lesléa Newman
Distant Music - Joan Annsfire
The Awful Suicidal Swans - Flower Conroy
Joy Street - Laura Foley
Chiaroscuro Kisses - G.L. Morrison
The Lillian Trilogy - Mary Meriam
Lady of the Moon - Amy Lowell, Lillian Faderman, Mary Meriam
Irresistible Sonnets - ed. Mary Meriam
Lavender Review - ed. Mary Meriam

www.ingramcontent.com/pod-product-compliance
Lightning Source LLC
Chambersburg PA
CBHW070039070426
42449CB00012BA/3093